Garfield gains weight

BY: JIM DAVIS

BALLANTINE BOOKS · NEW YORK

Copyright © 1981 by United Feature Syndicate, Inc.

All rights reserved under International and Pan-American Copyright Conventions. Published in the United States by Ballantine Books, a division of Random House, Inc., New York, and simultaneously in Canada by Random House of Canada Limited, Toronto, Canada.

Library of Congress Catalog Card Number: 80-69730

ISBN 0-345-32008-5

Manufactured in the United States of America

First Ballantine Books Edition: March 1981

50   49

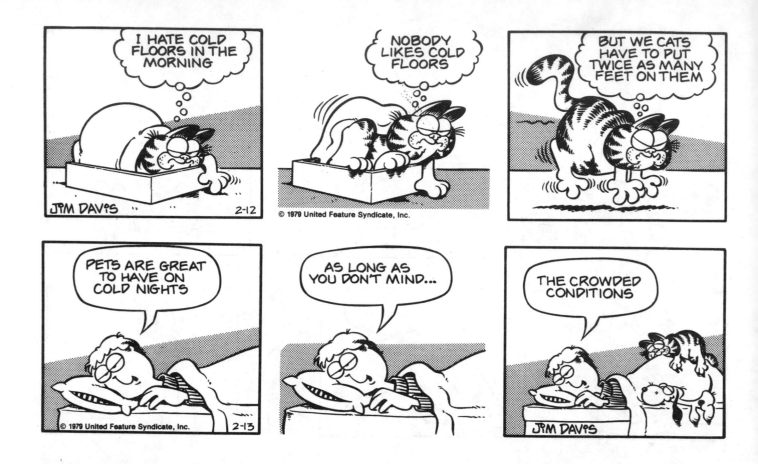

BE HONEST, POOKY. DO YOU THINK I'M GETTING A LITTLE PUDGY AROUND THE MIDDLE?

2-21

NOT A LOT OF PERSONALITY, BUT HE CERTAINLY KNOWS WHEN TO KEEP HIS MOUTH SHUT

JIM DAVIS

2-22

A DANCING BEAR?

NEXT TIME, I GET TO LEAD

© 1979 United Feature Syndicate, Inc. JIM DAVIS

HMMM, JON'S DRAWING BOARD. HMMM, SOME PAPER. HMMM, SOME INK

I THINK THIS WORLD WOULD BE A NICER PLACE IN WHICH TO LIVE: IF COUNTRIES COULD SETTLE THEIR DIFFERENCES WITHOUT HURTING ANYBODY. IF EVERYONE SMILED AT EVEN PEOPLE THEY DIDN'T KNOW

IF NOBODY HAD TO STEAL. IF PEOPLE LAUGHED MORE. IF EVERYONE FED THEIR CATS ALL THE LASAGNA THEY COULD EAT. IF WE ALL TOOK MORE PRIDE IN OUR HOMES AND OUR NEIGHBORHOODS

© 1979 United Feature Syndicate, Inc.

3-18

IF WE RESPECTED OUR SENIOR CITIZENS MORE. IF THERE WERE NO VIOLENCE IN MOVIES AND TELEVISION. IF EVERYONE COULD READ AND WRITE. IF FAMILIES TALKED MORE

IF FRIENDS HUGGED MORE. IF EVERYONE STOPPED AT LEAST ONCE A WEEK TO STROKE A CAT. AFTER ALL, WE'RE ALL IN THIS TOGETHER

HEY, GARFIELD

WHAT'S THIS?

OH, JUST SOME PAW PRINTS

JIM DAVIS

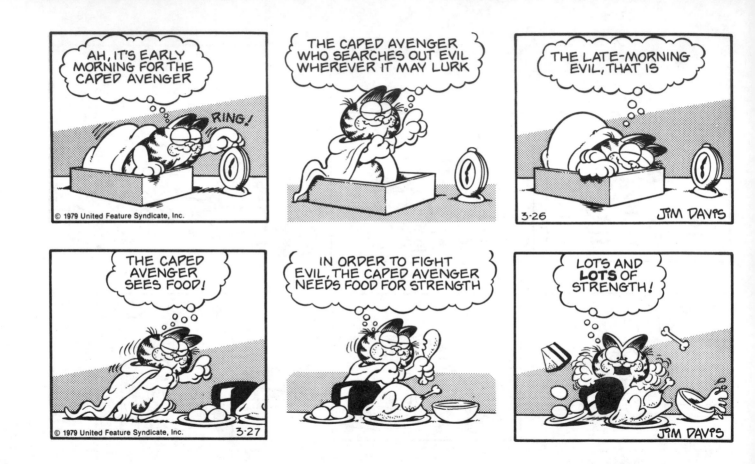

© 1979 United Feature Syndicate, Inc.

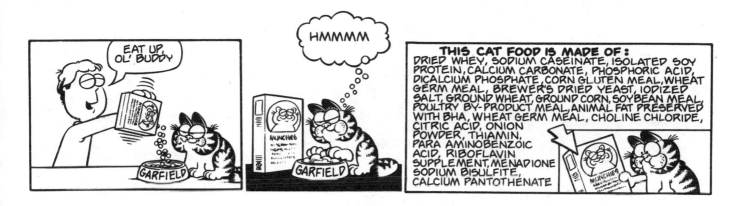

5-13 JIM DAVIS

© 1979 United Feature Syndicate, Inc.

DID I EVER TELL YOU ABOUT MY UNCLE HARRY? HE WAS A FAMOUS MOUSER AT A GLASS PLANT IN GAS CITY, INDIANA

5-23

© 1979 United Feature Syndicate, Inc.

LEGEND HAS IT THAT UNCLE HARRY CHASED A MOUSE RIGHT INTO TANK #2

NOW HE'S A PAPERWEIGHT IN BAYONNE, NEW JERSEY

JIM DAVIS

GRAB!

JIM DAVIS

BONK!

© 1979 United Feature Syndicate, Inc.

SMOOTH MOVE OL' BUDDY

HAVE YOU NO RESPECT FOR THE DEAD?

5-24

© 1979 United Feature Syndicate, Inc.

8-5

WHAT SAY I SWITCH OVER TO THE MOVIE, GANG?

NAH GRRR FFFT

JIM DAVIS

GARFIELD'S HISTORY OF CATS: A CAT DISCOVERED AMERICA!

IT WAS CHRISTOPHER COLUMBUS' CAT "BUCKEYE" WHO FIRST SPOTTED THE BEACH

PRIMARILY BECAUSE THE SANTA MARIA DIDN'T HAVE A SANDBOX

8-10

JIM DAVIS

© 1979 United Feature Syndicate, Inc.

GARFIELD'S HISTORY OF CATS: CATS' PENCHANT FOR SHARPENING THEIR CLAWS HAS SERVED MANY HISTORIC PURPOSES: IN VICTORIAN TIMES CATS WERE USED TO ANTIQUE FURNITURE

DURING THE SPANISH-AMERICAN WAR, CATS WERE USED AS INTERROGATORS

AND TODAY, THE POST OFFICE USES CATS TO SORT MAIL MARKED "FRAGILE"

RRRRRRR

8-11

I'LL TALK! I'LL TALK!

© 1979 United Feature Syndicate, Inc.

JIM DAVIS

A Talk with Jim Davis:
Most Asked Questions

How far in advance do you do the strip?

"Eight to ten weeks—no less, no more. I operate on what Al Capp termed 'the ragged edge of disaster.' "

When did GARFIELD first appear in newspapers?

"June 19, 1978."

Do you own a cat? A GARFIELD?

"No. My wife, Carolyn, is allergic to cats. However, I did grow up on a farm with about 25 cats."

Where do you get your ideas for the strip?

"I glean a lot of good ideas from fan mail. Cat owners are very proud of their cats and supply a generous amount of cat stories."

What GARFIELD products are on the market and in production?

"Books, calendars, T-shirts, coffee mugs, posters, tote bags, greeting cards, puzzles...in another few months GARFIELD will be on everything but pantyhose and TVs."

Why a cat?

"Aside from the obvious reasons, that I know and love cats, I noticed there were a lot of comic-strip dogs who were commanding their share of the comic pages but precious few cats. It seemed like a good idea."

Where did you get the name GARFIELD?

"My grandfather's name was James A. Garfield Davis. The name GARFIELD to me sounds like a fat cat...or a St. Bernard...or a neat line of thermal underwear."

What did you do for a living before GARFIELD?

"I was assistant on the comic strip TUMBLEWEEDS and a free-lance commercial artist."

What's your sign?

"Leo, of course, the sign of the cat."

Have you ever been convicted of a felony?

"Next question, please."

Are you subject to fainting spells, seizures, and palpitations?

"Only when I work."

Have you ever spent time in a mental institution?

"Yes, I visit my comics editor there."

Do you advocate the overthrow of our government by violent means?

"No, but I have given consideration to vandalizing my local license branch."

Are you hard of hearing?

"Huh?"

Do you wish to donate an organ?

"Heck no, but I have a piano I can let go cheap."